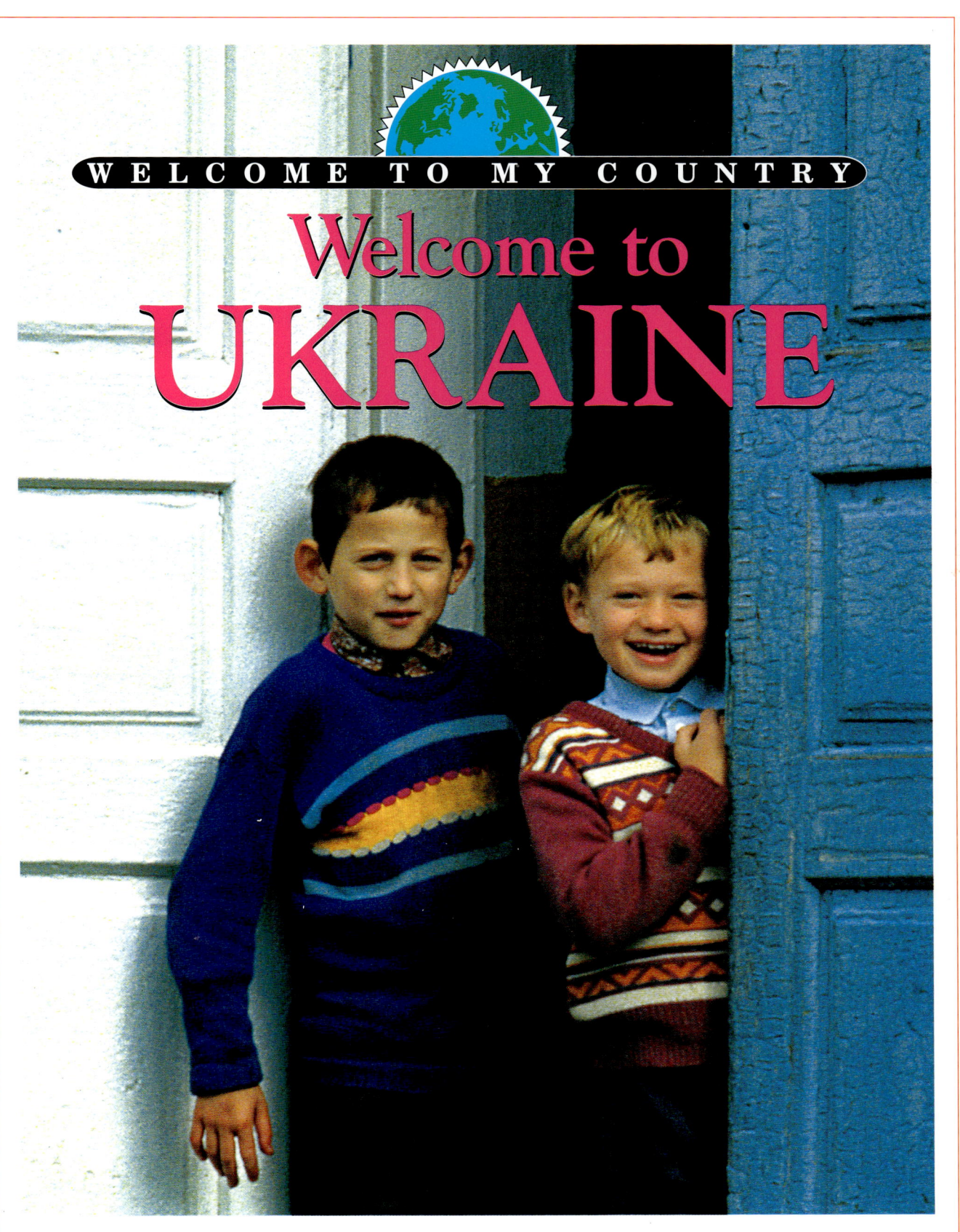

WELCOME TO MY COUNTRY

Welcome to
UKRAINE

Gareth Stevens Publishing
A WORLD ALMANAC EDUCATION GROUP COMPANY

Written by
KATHARINE BROWN/PAVEL ZEMLIANSKY

Edited by
MELVIN NEO

Edited in USA by
DOROTHY L. GIBBS

Designed by
GEOSLYN LIM

Picture research by
SUSAN JANE MANUEL

First published in North America in 2003 by
Gareth Stevens Publishing
A World Almanac Education Group Company
330 West Olive Street, Suite 100
Milwaukee, Wisconsin 53212 USA

Please visit our web site at:
www.garethstevens.com
For a free color catalog describing
Gareth Stevens Publishing's list of high-quality
books and multimedia programs,
call 1-800-542-2595 (USA) or
1-800-387-3178 (Canada).
Gareth Stevens Publishing's fax: (414) 332-3567.

© **TIMES MEDIA PRIVATE LIMITED 2003**
Originated and designed by
Times Editions
An imprint of Times Media Private Limited
A member of the Times Publishing Group
Times Centre, 1 New Industrial Road
Singapore 536196
http://www.timesone.com.sg/te

Library of Congress Cataloging-in-Publication Data
Brown, Katharine Elizabeth, 1972–
Welcome to Ukraine / Katharine Brown and Pavel Zemliansky.
p. cm. — (Welcome to my country)
Contents: Welcome to Ukraine! — The land — History —
Government and the economy — People and lifestyle —
Language — Arts — Leisure — Food.
Includes bibliographical references and index.
ISBN 0-8368-2555-1 (lib. bdg.)
1. Ukraine—Juvenile literature. [1. Ukraine.]
I. Zemliansky, Pavel. II. Title. III. Series.
DK508.515.B76   2003
947.7—dc21   2003042747

Printed in Singapore

1 2 3 4 5 6 7 8 9 07 06 05 04 03

PICTURE CREDITS
A.N.A. Press Agency: 4, 6, 9, 25, 34
Art Directors & TRIP Photo Library:
    3 (center), 11, 18, 24, 36, 41
Jan Butchofsky/Houserstock: cover
Camera Press: 1
Tania D'Avignon: 2, 3 (top), 3 (bottom),
    7, 8, 10, 15 (top), 16, 17, 20 (bottom),
    29, 31, 32, 33, 38, 39, 40, 44, 45
Focus Team — Italy: 21, 28
Getty Images/Hulton Archive: 12, 13,
    20 (top), 27
The Hutchison Library: 5, 14, 19, 22, 23,
    30, 35
Topham Picturepoint: 15 (bottom), 26, 37

Digital Scanning by Superskill Graphics Pte Ltd

Contents

Words that appear in the glossary are printed in **boldface** type the first time they occur in the text.

121928

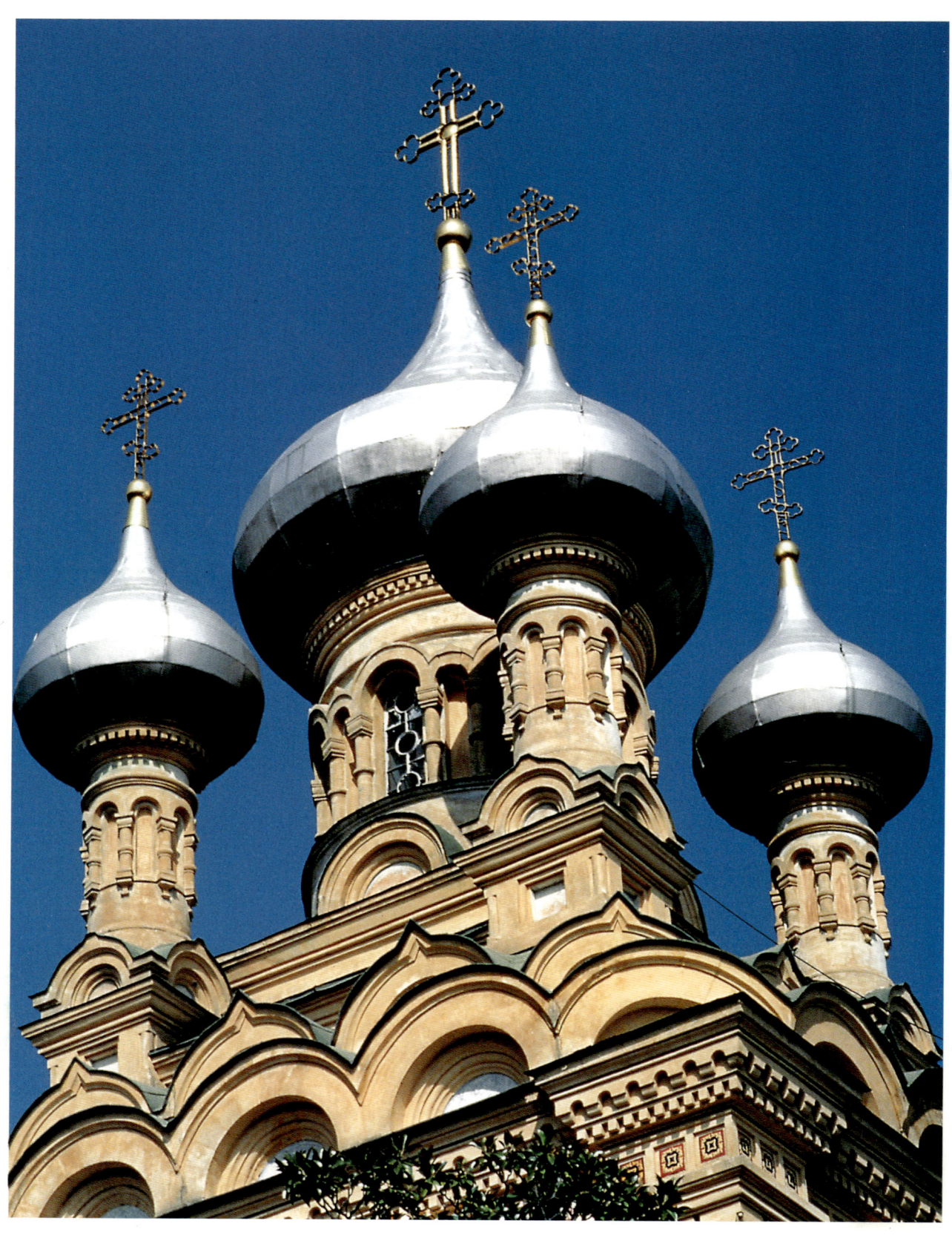

Welcome to Ukraine!

Located in Eastern Europe, Ukraine is the second-largest country on the European continent. Although, for centuries, it had been controlled by many powerful peoples and nations, Ukraine finally gained independence in 1991. Let's explore Ukraine and learn about its history and culture.

Opposite: Onion-shaped domes are a common part of the architecture of many churches in Ukraine. These domes are on an Eastern Orthodox church in Yalta.

Below: Ukraine's rich soil is good for farming. Agriculture is a big part of the country's economy.

The Flag of Ukraine

The Ukrainian flag has a blue band at the top and a yellow band at the bottom. Blue stands for the sky. Yellow represents the country's golden fields. This flag was first used in 1848, then reappeared after Ukraine's independence.

The Land

Ukraine has an area of 233,089 square miles (603,700 square kilometers). It shares its borders on the west and the southwest with the countries of Poland, Slovakia, Hungary, Romania, and Moldova. Belarus is to the north, and Russia is to the east and northeast. The southern coast is on the Black Sea, the southeastern coast on the Sea of Azov.

Below: Except for mountain areas in the west and the south, most of Ukraine is flat, fertile grasslands called steppes.

The Carpathian Mountains stretch across parts of western Ukraine and into Poland, Slovakia, and Romania. At 6,762 feet (2,061 meters), Mount Hoverla, in the Carpathian range, is the country's highest peak.

The Crimean Mountains form the only other mountain range in Ukraine. They are located in the south, on the Crimean **Peninsula**, which is one of the most beautiful parts of the country. This region's warm climate is good for growing fruit, and its sunny beaches on the Black Sea have made it a popular vacation area.

Climate

Temperatures in Ukraine can be very hot in summer and very cold in winter, depending on the part of the country. Normal summer temperatures average 68° Fahrenheit (20° Celsius) in Kiev, which is located in northern Ukraine, and 75° F (24° C) on the southern Crimean Peninsula. Average winter temperatures are 21° F (–6° C) in Kiev and 39° F (4° C) on the peninsula.

Below: Winters in southern Ukraine are usually rainy and mild, but snow falls frequently in northern areas, especially in the Carpathian range.

Plants and Animals

Northern Ukraine has thick oak and maple forests. Eastern and western areas also have many trees. Except for **vineyards** and peach orchards along its southern coast, the hot, dry Crimean Peninsula has mostly low, thin shrubs.

Elk, deer, and wild pigs are some of the more common animals found in Ukraine. Wild sheep and muskrats, which, at one time, had completely disappeared, have now been brought back to Ukrainian habitats.

Above: Animals such as bison and wild horses used to roam freely in Ukraine. Now they are found only in national parks and nature **reserves**.

History

In about 4000 B.C., the Trypillians, who were mainly farmers, settled in the western and central parts of what is now Ukraine. Around 800 B.C., the **nomadic**, warlike Scythians moved in. After the Scythians came Sarmatians, Goths, Huns, Bulgars, Avars, Turkic Khazars, and Magyars. Especially from A.D. 200 to 900, many foreign **civilizations** ruled Ukraine.

Left: The Scythians were known for the huge stone statues of women they built across Ukraine's countryside. Some of these statues, called babas, are still standing today.

The Kievan Rus and Galicia

Between the ninth and the thirteenth centuries, Ukraine was ruled by the Kievan Rus, which is considered the country's greatest ancient civilization. Ukrainians and Russians both believe that this kingdom started the cultures of their peoples. In the 1200s, however, the center of Ukrainian society and politics moved to the western side of the country, and Ukraine became part of the kingdom of Galicia.

Above: The Kyevo Pecherska Lavra monastery, in Kiev, was built during the reign of the Kievan Rus.

More Foreign Rule

By the 1300s, Poland, Lithuania, and descendants of Mongol tribes all ruled parts of Ukraine. Poland **annexed** the areas controlled by Lithuania in 1569, but Mongols continued to rule Crimea. In 1654, Ukrainian **Kozaks** asked the Russian Empire to help end Polish rule. Instead of gaining its independence, however, much of Ukraine became part of the Russian Empire.

Above: In 1918, Russia signed the Treaty of Brest-Litovsk, making several countries under its control, including Ukraine, independent. The treaty, however, was **abolished** at the end of World War I, so Russian rule continued.

A Soviet Republic

After the Russian Revolution of 1917, Ukraine formed its own government and elected a president. Because of fighting within the country, however, the new **republic** did not last long.

In 1922, Ukraine became one of the fifteen republics that made up the **Soviet Union**. For a period of time during World War II, the Germans occupied Ukraine, but Russia quickly regained control at the end of the war.

Below: During World War II, many Ukrainian homes were destroyed in battles between Germany and the Soviet Union.

An Independent Nation

The Soviet Union started breaking up in 1990. On August 24, 1991, Ukraine declared its independence. The main goal of the country's new government was to improve its poor economy. In spite of programs to make industries more productive and the country more **prosperous**, Ukraine's cost of living has increased, and the gap between rich and poor has become wider.

Above: In 1990, many Ukrainians gathered in Kiev to demand Ukraine's independence from the Soviet Union.

Princess Olga (890–969)

After the death of her husband, Igor I of Kiev, in 945, Princess Olga ruled the Kievan Rus kingdom for twenty-one years. Olga became the first saint of the Russian Orthodox Church.

Princess Olga

Bohdan Khmelnytsky (1595–1657)

Kozak leader Bohdan Khmelnytsky organized a revolt, in 1648, to end Polish rule in Ukraine. In 1654, he asked the Russian Empire for help. The Russians invaded Poland, then gradually took control of Ukraine.

Stepan Bandera (1909–1959)

As the leader of the Organization of Ukrainian **Nationalists**, Stepan Bandera was against Soviet control of Ukraine. During World War II, he and his followers fought against both Germany and the Soviet Union.

Stepan Bandera

Government and the Economy

Ukraine is a democratic republic led by a president who is elected by the people. The president appoints a prime minister and **deputy** prime ministers to assist in running the government. These appointments are approved by Ukraine's parliament, which is called Verkhovna Rada.

Below: Verkhovna Rada, which is the lawmaking branch of the Ukrainian government, meets in the capital city of Kiev.

The Verkhovna Rada, or Supreme Council, has 450 members. Like the president, members of the Verkhovna Rada are elected by the people. Each member serves a four-year term.

Ukraine has twenty-four oblasts, or local divisions of government, plus the **autonomous** republic of Kryms'ka, on the Crimean Peninsula.

Industry

Industries, especially mining and metal processing, are very important to the Ukrainian economy. The Donets Basin is the center of industrial production.

It is also Ukraine's coal mining center. While coal is the main natural resource, the country also has large deposits of iron ore, which is used to make steel. Besides being a major steel producer, Ukraine manufactures transportation equipment and chemical products. Food is another important industry.

Above: Ukraine is a world leader in metallurgy, which is the process of separating metal from its ore so it can be used to make **alloys** and metal products.

Agriculture

Large areas of Ukraine have rich, black soil that is ideal for agriculture. Grains, especially wheat, and sugar beets are the country's most important crops.

Ukraine also grows fruit. The Crimean Peninsula is known for its vineyards, and central and eastern Ukraine have apple and cherry orchards. Until 1991, Ukrainian farms were large and owned by the state. Today, private households run small farms, and many Ukrainians grow their own fruits and vegetables.

Above: Working in the fields became much easier after Ukrainian farmers were equipped with modern machinery. Besides wheat and sugar beets, crops include barley, rice, corn, and potatoes.

People and Lifestyle

About 73 percent of the people in Ukraine are Ukrainians. Another 22 percent are of Russian **ancestry**. The remaining population belongs to minority groups, which include Poles, Romanians, Crimean Tatars, and Belorussians.

Above: In the 1940s and 1950s, the Soviet Union drove the Tatars out of Crimea and forced them to move to Central Asia and Siberia. The Tatars began coming back to Crimea in the early 1990s.

Left: Due to their country's location between Europe and Asia, many Ukrainians have a mixed **heritage**.

People living in the eastern parts of Ukraine have been influenced by the culture of nearby Russia, and most of them speak the Russian language. Most of the people in western Ukraine speak Ukrainian, although many of them also know Russian.

The most heavily populated areas of Ukraine are the eastern Donets Basin, the city of Kiev, and several other large cities, such as Kharkov and L'viv.

Above: Although many Ukrainians have moved to the cities, countryside villages are still a big part of the nation's culture. Villagers treasure old customs and pass traditions on to new generations.

Family Life

Most families in Ukraine are small, with only two or three children. For traditional and economic reasons, both parents usually have jobs. In Ukrainian culture, wives are encouraged to work outside the home so they do not have to depend on their husbands for financial support. Men retire from their jobs at the age of sixty, while women can stop working at the age of fifty-five.

Left: Especially since Ukraine became independent, its people cannot afford to have many children.

In Ukraine's cities, most families live in small apartments. In villages, families have separate houses and usually have more space. They also have plots of land for growing fresh fruits and vegetables.

In both cities and villages, however, Ukrainians buy most of their food at markets. They also have grocery stores, called *hastronom* (hahs-troh-NOHM), for day-to-day shopping.

Above: Markets are the most popular places to buy food in Ukraine because the food is fresher, and the prices are often lower than at a grocery store.

Education

Since becoming independent, Ukraine has been reforming education. In the past, all education was free, and the schools were run by the state. Today, Ukrainian children can attend either state-run schools, which are still free, or private schools, which charge a fee. Also, since independence, schools all over the country now teach Ukrainian history, language, and culture.

Only high school graduates who have passed the required entrance examinations may attend a university or one of Ukraine's institutes, which are colleges of specialized study in fields such as medicine, engineering, or the arts. Most higher education programs in Ukraine last five years. Upon completion, students receive diplomas of higher education, which are more advanced than the bachelor's degrees for four-year programs.

Below:
These students are attending a class at Kyiv Polytechnic Institute. For higher education, most of the large cities in Ukraine have a university and one or more institutes.

Religion

Christianity is Ukraine's main religion. In the eastern and central parts of the country, most Christians belong to the Ukrainian Orthodox or the Ukrainian Autonomous Orthodox faiths. Most of the Christians in western Ukraine are either Eastern Rite or Roman Catholics.

Above:
These Ukrainians are celebrating an Eastern Orthodox religious service. Other Christian faiths in Ukraine include Baptist, Pentecostal, and Evangelical. The country also has Muslim and Jewish communities.

During **communist** rule, when the country was part of the Soviet Union, many Ukrainian churches were closed, and church leaders were sent away or put in prison to discourage religious practice. Since independence, however, Ukrainians have a renewed interest in religion. Today, religious groups play very important roles, including running schools and raising money for charity.

Left:
Roman Catholic Pope John Paul II visited Ukraine for the first time in June 2001. During his visit, he led this outdoor service in the city of L'viv.

Language

After centuries of Russian rule and influence, Ukrainian nationalists are proud to speak the Ukrainian language. Most of the population, however, speaks both Ukrainian and Russian, and the country's schools still teach the Russian language.

Part of the Eastern Slavic language group, Ukrainian is closely related to Russian but with its own grammar and sounds. It has also borrowed words from the Tatar and Turkish languages.

Left: The signs on these telephone booths are written in **Cyrillic** script. This alphabet was invented in 861 by two monks, Cyril and Methodius, who later became Christian saints. Ukrainians write their language in Cyrillic script.

Literature

Taras Shevchenko is Ukraine's most famous writer. He wrote poems that promoted Ukrainian independence and nationalism. Other patriotic poets from Ukraine include Ivan Franko (1856–1916), who also wrote prose about western Ukraine, and Lesya Ukrayinka (1871–1913), who also wrote folk plays. Novelist Mykhaylo Kotsyubynsky (1864–1913) is another important Ukrainian writer.

Arts

Ukrainians are very creative. Their art combines folk traditions and European techniques into original forms that are enjoyed by a variety of audiences.

Left: This stringed instrument is called a *bandura* (bahn-DOO-rah). It is a modern version of Ukraine's oldest folk instrument, the *kobza* (KAHB-zah). The kobza was a stringed instrument played long ago by traveling musicians known as *kobzari* (kahb-zah-REE). All kobzari were blind. Led by guides, they moved from village to village playing music and singing folk songs.

Music and Dance

Everyone in Ukraine enjoys folk songs and dances, and many Ukrainians are members of **amateur** song and dance groups. Performances by professional folk groups at concerts and festivals are always well attended. Kiev's Veryovka Ukrainian Folk Choir is a professional folk group that sings and dances all over the world. Pop music, especially by Western performers, is the favorite style of most young Ukrainians.

Theater

All of the large cities in Ukraine have professional theater groups. Many of these cities have one theater that stages only Russian plays and another theater that stages only Ukrainian plays. A new theater in Kiev, called Koleso, is becoming famous for its lively young actors, who often invite members of the audience to join them on the stage.

Left: Cities in Ukraine that have professional ballet companies include Kiev, Kharkov, L'viv, and Odesa.

Painted Eggs

Making *pysanky* (pes un kee), which are brightly painted Easter eggs, is a popular Ukrainian craft and, perhaps, the country's best-known art form. The eggs are decorated by hand using melted wax and colored dyes. First, a design is drawn on an eggshell with wax. Then, the eggshell is dipped into dye. The dye will not color any part of the eggshell that has wax on it.

Above: Pysanky are decorated with colorful designs in many different patterns. Each design has its own special meaning.

Leisure

Ukrainians are warm, **sociable** people, who like to spend their leisure time with family and friends. Events such as birthdays and weddings are long

celebrations with many guests and lots of food, music, and dancing. In cities and towns, especially on weekends, people gather at parks to relax or to play chess or soccer.

Above: Whether they are in a classroom or a city park or café, young Ukrainians enjoy time spent with friends.

During July or August, many Ukrainians like to take a vacation. Recently, winter ski trips have also become popular. Most Ukrainians take only one vacation a year, but it is often ten to twenty days long.

Below: Its seaside location makes the Crimean Peninsula, in southern Ukraine, one of the most popular places for a summer vacation.

Many Ukrainians in the cities own summerhouses where they can spend their vacations. Families who cannot afford to travel usually spend vacation time relaxing at home or on the beach.

Newspapers and Television

Before 1991, Ukrainians kept up with the news by reading magazines and newspapers. After the breakup of the Soviet Union, television became the main source of news. All parts of Ukraine receive television broadcasts from several Ukrainian stations. The eastern areas also get Russian stations. Besides television, large cities each have about a dozen radio stations.

Above:
When television became available to Ukrainians, in the 1990s, sales of magazines and newspapers rapidly declined. Since then, print media have regained their popularity.

Sports

Soccer is Ukraine's most popular sport. Thousands of fans attend Ukrainian Premier League games every weekend. Other favorite sports include track and field and gymnastics. Athletes from Ukraine have won championships and medals in European, Olympic, and world competitions.

Below: Andriy Shevchenko is a Ukrainian soccer star. In the 1999–2000 season, he was the top scorer in the Italian Series A league.

Holidays and Festivals

Since regaining religious freedom, Ukrainians are able to celebrate Christmas. Soviet rule discouraged the celebration of Christmas because it is a religious holiday. Today, it is becoming Ukraine's most popular and colorful winter festival. Because of the calendar used by the Ukrainian Orthodox Church, however, Christmas in Ukraine falls on January 7.

Below:
On Christmas Eve, Ukrainian children go from house to house singing *kolyadky* (koh-LJAHD-kee), which are like Christmas carols. People in the houses usually reward the children with candy treats or money.

Before Christmas became such a popular holiday in Ukraine, the New Year was the main winter celebration. January 1 is still an important day for most Ukrainians. Many celebrate New Year's Eve with large parties, street parades, and fireworks. Malanka, on January 13, is New Year's Eve on the Orthodox calendar. It is a folk holiday that usually ends the Christmas season.

Above: In Ukraine, flowers are part of every spring holiday celebration, including Easter.

Food

Ukraine is an agricultural country, so Ukrainian cooking uses a lot of grain and other foods that are grown locally. In summer, people eat plenty of fresh fruits and vegetables. For winter, they **preserve** many fruits and vegetables.

Favorite foods include potato dishes and *borsch* (bohrsh), which is a cold soup made with cabbage, tomatoes, and beets. If beef is added, it is served hot.

Above: Because Ukraine grows a lot of wheat and other grains, bread is a very popular food.

Holubtsi (hoh-loob-TSI) is another Ukrainian favorite. It is ground beef and rice wrapped in cabbage leaves and served with thick gravy. Ukraine's national dish is *varenyky* (vah-REH-nee-kee), which are dumplings filled with almost anything, from cabbage to cottage cheese to strawberries.

Below: Bowls of borsch are usually the first course of a main meal. During the week, the main meal is served in the evening, on weekends, in the middle of the day.

At the end of a meal, Ukrainians enjoy drinking tea or coffee. Desserts are usually made with fried or baked dough. Pies and cakes are popular, too.

E F

N

	National Boundary
	Oblast Boundary
■	Capital
●	City
∿	River

RUSSIA

● Kharkov

KHARKIVS'KA

LUHANS'KA

Donets Basin

DNIPROPETROVS'KA

DONETS'KA

ZAPORIZ'KA

SEA OF AZOV

Crimean Peninsula

Crimean Mountains

Yalta

RUSSIA

Belarus A1–D1
Black Sea C4–F5

Carpathian Mountains A2–B4
Cherkas'ka Oblast C3–D3
Chernihivs'ka Oblast D1–D2
Chernivets'ka Oblast B3
Crimean Mountains E5
Crimean Peninsula D4–E5

Dnipro River C1–D4
Dnipropetrovs'ka Oblast D3–E3
Donets Basin F3
Donets'ka Oblast E3–F3

Hungary A3

Ivano-Frankivs'ka Oblast A3–B3

Kharkivs'ka Oblast E2–E3
Kharkov E2
Khersons'ka Oblast D3–E4
Khmel'nyts'ka Oblast B2–B3
Kiev C2
Kirovohrads'ka Oblast C3–D3
Kryms'ka Autonomous Republic D4–E5
Kyyivs'ka Oblast C2–C3

Luhans'ka Oblast F2–F3
L'viv A2
L'vivs'ka Oblast A3–B2

Moldova B3–C4
Moryntsi C3
Mount Hoverla A3
Mykolayivs'ka Oblast C3–D4

Odesa C4
Odes'ka Oblast C3–D4

Poland A1–A2
Poltavs'ka Oblast D2–E3

Rivnens'ka Oblast B1–B2
Romania A3–C5
Russia D1–F5

Sea of Azov E4–F4
Slovakia A2–A3
Sums'ka Oblast D1–E2

Ternopils'ka Oblast B2–B3

Vinnyts'ka Oblast B3–C3
Volyns'ka Oblast A1–B2

Yalta E5

Zakarpats'ka Oblast A3
Zaporiz'ka Oblast E3–F4
Zhytomyrs'ka Oblast B2–C2

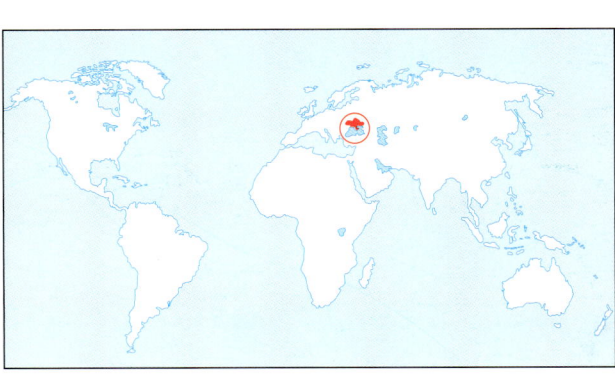

Quick Facts

Official Name Ukraine

Capital Kiev

Official Language Ukrainian

Population 48 396,470 million (July 2002 estimate)

Land Area 233,089 square miles (603,700 square km)

Administrative Districts (Oblasts) Cherkas'ka, Chernihivs'ka, Chernivets'ka, Dnipropetrovs'ka, Donets'ka, Ivano-Frankivs'ka, Kharkivs'ka, Khersons'ka, Khmel'nyts'ka, Kirovohrads'ka, Kyyivs'ka, Luhans'ka, L'vivs'ka, Mykolayivs'ka, Odes'ka, Poltavs'ka, Rivnens'ka, Sums'ka, Ternopils'ka, Vinnyts'ka, Volyns'ka, Zakarpats'ka, Zaporiz'ka, Zhytomyrs'ka, and Kryms'ka (the autonomous republic of Crimea)

Highest Point Mount Hoverla 6,762 feet (2,061 m)

Major Mountains Carpathian, Crimean

Main Religions Catholic, Eastern Orthodox

Currency Hryvnia (5.3 UAH = U.S. $1 as of 2003)

Opposite: The city of Yalta lies at the foot of the Crimean Mountains.

Glossary

abolished: ended, cancelled, or done away with.

alloys: metals that are made by mixing two or more base metals together with other nonmetal elements.

amateur: not professional, performing an activity for enjoyment rather than for money.

ancestry: a line of family members from past generations.

annexed: added a country or territory to the existing territory of the controlling country or state.

autonomous: self-governing.

civilizations: highly developed societies with established governments and cultures and written histories.

communist: related to a political system in which the government owns and controls all goods and resources.

Cyrillic: an alphabet based on Greek symbols and used in writing Russian, Ukrainian, and other languages of Eastern Europe and Asia.

deputy: officially appointed or elected to serve as an assistant.

heritage: the customs and traditions passed down by earlier generations.

Kozaks: rebellious Ukrainian peasants who became independent soldiers and fought to end Polish rule.

nationalists: people who are devoted and loyal to their country.

nomadic: wandering or moving around without having a permanent home.

peninsula: a long strip of land that is surrounded by water on three sides.

preserve: to prepare food by pickling it or cooking it with sugar so it will not spoil during a long period of storage.

prosperous: economically successful.

rallies: large gatherings of people to support a common cause.

republic: a nation in which citizens elect their own government representatives.

reserves: areas of protected land that are used only for special purposes, such as preserving nature.

sociable: friendly; seeking to be in the company of others.

Soviet Union: a communist nation that dissolved in 1991 and had included Russia and fourteen other Slavic republics.

vineyards: areas of land where grapevines are planted.

More Books to Read

The Bird's Gift: A Ukrainian Easter Story. Eric A. Kimmel (Holiday House)

Enough. Marsha Forchuk Skrypuch (Fitzhenry and Whiteside)

I Am Eastern Orthodox. Religions of the World series. Philemon D. Sevastiades (Powerkids Press)

The Old Man's Mitten: A Ukrainian Tale. Yevonne Pollock (Mondo)

Ukraine. Ancient and Living Cultures series. Christine Ronan (Goodyear)

Ukraine. Festivals of the World series. Vladimir Bassis (Gareth Stevens)

Ukraine: A New Independence. Exploring Cultures of the World series. Rebecca Clay (Benchmark Books)

Ukraine: Sasha Kotyenko's Painting "Embroidery Time." Young Artists of the World series. Jacquiline Touba (Rosen)

Ukrainian Egg Decoration: A Holiday Tradition. Crafts of the World series. Ann Stalcup (Powerkids Press)

Videos

From Kiev to the Crimea: Along the Dnipro and the Black Sea. (Volodymyr Kuzyk)

Ukrainian Power. (Ukrainian Power Videos, Inc.)

Web Sites

ukraine.uazone.net

www.infoukes.com/culture/

www.pysanka.com

www.ukraine.online.com.ua

Due to the dynamic nature of the Internet, some web sites stay current longer than others. To find additional web sites, use a reliable search engine with one or more of the following keywords to help you locate information about Ukraine. Keywords: *bandura, Carpathian Mountains, Kharkov, Kiev, Kozaks, Malanka, Yalta.*

Index